PUTTING ON THE SPIRIT

Ten Minute Devotions for Busy Moms

Katie Hornor

What others are saying about Putting On the Spirit

"I thoroughly enjoyed Putting on the Spirit. The devotions in this book are short enough for any busy mother to fit them into her day and yet thought provoking enough to stay with her all day long!"
Jennifer Green, Missionary to the deaf of Yucatan, Mexico and mother of four grown children

"Putting on the Spirit is a really good devotional book. One I can wholeheartedly promote! And I love that is has a free workbook to go along with it!"
Missy Priebe, Dot to Dot Connections

"Putting on the Spirit is so inspiring and encouraging! I am SUCH a busy mom and I love the guidance that Katie gives and the fact that she is a homeschooling, busy mom, too."
Lyn Parker - Super Mom Illusion

Putting On the Spirit: Ten-Minute Devotions for Busy Moms

by Katie Hornor, www.ParadisePraises.com

The Audio Book Version and a free companion workbook for this study is available via download at http://paradisepraises.com/putting-on-the-spirit.

Table of Contents

Foreword

Every mom with children at home is busy. We're busy with our children. We're busy managing our homes. Our husbands need our care and attention. Work calls. Our parents need us. On and on it goes. It's easy to become weary and burned out in all of this busyness.

Everywhere I have spoken in the past several years, I have met moms who are barely hanging on. The pressure of thinking we have to measure up to someone else's standard can be overwhelming. I know. I've been there.

Being busy is not the problem. The problem is that we don't take the time out of our busy schedules for what really matters. The most important thing we can do each day is to nourish our spirit by spending just a few of our precious minutes alone with the Lord.

In *Putting On the Spirit*, Katie Hornor reminds busy moms of where grace for the journey can be found: at the feet of Jesus. God's Word is a love letter to every busy mom. Katie is right: just ten minutes can change you from the inside out. Take the challenge, busy mom. Put on the Spirit and let him show you how to plan your days.

Heidi St. John
Wife and Mother of Seven
Author and Speaker
www.thebusymom.com

Introduction

I know what it's like to be busy. I've even been referred to as a supermom. But in my busyness, I often wish I had time to sit for hours with my cup of coffee or tea and drink in the Scriptures. The fact is that in this season of life, with four small children, those times are few and far between. Too often I find myself grabbing a quick verse here and there, donning my Supermom cape of "I can do this," without even asking God for his help, and rushing on about my day.

I know I should be putting on the Spirit instead of robing myself in the cape of my own strength, but I just don't have the time. With diapers and dishes and homeschooling and meal planning and grocery shopping and church activities and work deadlines and . . . well, you get the picture. If I'm going to put on the Spirit, I need something that gives me a daily dose of the Word, that encourages me, that challenges me, and that *doesn't take very long*.

If you can identify with what you have just read, hope is on its way.

When I began to realize that my own "superpowers" weren't cutting it and began to look seriously for the time to put on the Spirit, I found it. And you can too.

You and I are very busy moms, but we do have time for the Word in small increments—waiting for the kids in the carpool line, nursing the baby, waiting at sports or instrument practice, during nap time, during lunch break at work, just before dinner, or just after putting the kids down for the night. It is possible for each of us to find ten minutes a day to spend with the Lord, clothing ourselves in his Spirit.

This one-month study, *Putting On the Spirit*, and its companion workbook are especially designed by me, a busy mom, for you, a busy mom. With just ten minutes a day we will study all the fruit of the Spirit in one month (twenty-eight days plus three flex days). We'll take it one fruit at a time, but ultimately we'll see how all the fruit comes together and works as a whole to make us more like Christ. We'll also see how laying down our Supermom capes of insensitivity, pride, control, fleshly strength, and other sins in order to put on the fruit of the Spirit really *is* the best thing we can do, both for ourselves and for our families.

As you go through the study and look at various passages of Scripture, if you come to a word that you don't understand from the context of the verse, I encourage you to look up the meaning in a Bible dictionary. If you don't have one in your Bible or at home, you can go online to Blue Letter Bible or to your favorite online Bible dictionary and look up the words.

You will be writing something almost every day. You may be tempted to skip the writing parts, but I encourage you not to. I believe the writing will assist in internalizing and processing what you are learning. You may choose to write out the verses and answer the questions in your own Bible study notebook, or you may want to visit http://paradisepraises.com/putting-on-the-spirit and print out the free companion workbook for this study. The workbook has plenty of room for recording the verses and your thoughts.

So how about it? Are you ready to exchange your Supermom cape for something better? Will you commit to those precious ten minutes in your day and join me for this life-changing study of the fruit of the Spirit? It doesn't have to be the same place or time every day. It can be with coffee or without. If you miss a day, don't worry—just jump back in the next day. Claim your ten-minute quiet time whenever and wherever you can. You *can* do it! And I know you're going to be blessed!

Katie Hornor

Putting On Love: Day 1

But the fruit of the Spirit is **LOVE***, joy, peace, longsuffering, gentleness, goodness, faith, meekness, temperance: against such there is no law.* (Galatians 5:22–23)

The modern superheroes in the stories we have grown up with have a way of always coming out on top, always knowing just what to do in the nick of time to save the day. They are loved by most people, but in spite of all of their heroic efforts for the common good, they slip away before those who really want to *know and love* them get that chance.

It's time we Supermoms lay down our capes of untouchableness and put on the Spirit. It's time for us to really *love* and let ourselves *be loved.*

Right now, take some time to read 1 Corinthians 13:1–13 and really think through and pray over this passage. If you like to make notes in your Bible, I encourage you to mark each action and/or characteristic of love as you read. (The King James Version uses the word *charity* for love in this passage.)

Then finish your quiet time by asking God to show you how this love should look in your daily interactions with your family.

Putting On Love: Day 2

But the fruit of the Spirit is **LOVE**, *joy, peace, longsuffering, gentleness, goodness, faith, meekness, temperance: against such there is no law.* (Galatians 5:22–23)

Yesterday we read and prayed over 1 Corinthians 13:1–13, which is known almost universally as "the love chapter" of the Bible. The word translated *love* in Galatians 5:22 and the word translated *charity* in 1 Corinthians 13 are both a form of the Greek word *agape*. *Agape* is selfless, sacrificial, unconditional love—the highest type of love mentioned in the Bible.

Today, we're going to dig into this topic a little deeper. Here's how:

1. Get out a pen and your Bible study notebook or workbook.
2. Write out 1 Corinthians 13:1-13, verse by verse, in your own words. For instance, if you wanted to tell someone about this passage but didn't have your Bible handy, how would you express it? Paraphrase it.
3. Take a few minutes to pray over and answer these questions:
   a. What does this passage tell you about yourself?
   b. What does this passage tell you about God (about his character)?

Putting On Love: Day 3

But the fruit of the Spirit is **LOVE***, joy, peace, longsuffering, gentleness, goodness, faith, meekness, temperance: against such there is no law.* (Galatians 5:22–23)

1 Corinthians 13:1–13 explains *agape* love in pretty clear language. Here is how I understand love:

> Love:
> is longsuffering and patient
> is kind
> does not envy
> does not boast of itself
> is not prideful
> does not behave inappropriately, does not cause a scene
> is not selfish
> is not easily angered
> gives the benefit of the doubt, does not imagine evil against another
> does not rejoice in wrongdoing, sinful behavior, or the consequences of another
> rejoices in the truth and in Truth
> loves in spite of the circumstances
> never stops believing
> never gives up hope
> endures all, is constant

is faithful, consistent, dependable

In each of its characteristics mentioned here, love is an action. Therefore, I know that it must be possible to distinguish between love (the feeling) and love (the action).

Love *is* an action. The feeling we call *love* is the result of either performing the action ourselves or being the recipients of the action.

Love can be communicated through words, through spending time with someone, through doing something for someone, through tenderness and touch, through listening. Love uses so many languages!

So how does this apply to you and me as moms?

1. It's time to stop hiding behind the cape of "gotta cross everything off my list today." It's time to put on love (an action) and take time to read that book or play that game with your child.

2. It's time to take off the cape of Supermom envy and look for a way to bless that neighbor who appears to have it all together.

3. It's time to resist the urge to grow angry with your children or husband when things don't go as you want them to.

4. It's time to ask God to help you love in spite of your circumstances and in spite of your own plans being foiled.

When you decide (consciously choose) to love *whom* God loves in the *way* that he loves, I guarantee that your story will be epic.

Being clothed in his Spirit is so much better than any cape or hero's disguise the flesh can design.

Take a few minutes right now to ask the Lord to help you lay aside the Supermom cape of _____ (you fill in the blank) and really show his *love in action* to your family today and in the days to come.

Putting On Joy: Day 4

But the fruit of the Spirit is love, **JOY***, peace, longsuffering, gentleness, goodness, faith, meekness, temperance: against such there is no law.* (Galatians 5:22–23)

All of us wish we could be real Supermoms—never a to-do list we can't conquer, never a problem we can't solve, always strong enough to handle whatever crisis arises and come out on top. But if we're going to be super in God's eyes, we must choose joy. Why? Because Scripture says the joy of the Lord is our strength (Nehemiah 8:10).

"But," you may ask, "how do I find and put on joy in the everyday routine of laundry, child-training, housecleaning, dish washing, grocery shopping, meal planning, budget watching, and 101 other things on my Supermom to-do list?"

Today let's just examine two ways to put on joy. You will need your notebook or workbook.

1. There is joy in spending time with your Savior.

Look up and write out Psalm 16:11.

Choosing to spend time, even only a few concentrated minutes each day, hearing from God through his Word and talking with him through prayer lays the foundation for a peaceful heart and a joyful attitude throughout the day.

I know you're busy. I am too. Remember, time with God doesn't have to be the first thing in the morning. The important thing is not *when* you do it, but *that* you do it. Fellowship with our Creator and Savior always brings joy.

2. **There is joy in pondering salvation.**

Read Psalm 35:9, Psalm 95:1, and Isaiah 61:10.

Considering all that God has done for us by offering salvation, redemption, and adoption free of charge brings joy. The Scripture is full of references to finding joy in our salvation and in the God of our salvation. *Choosing* to dwell on this undeserved salvation brings joy.

Spend the last few minutes of your quiet time today praising and thanking God for his Son, and for his great and undeserved gift of salvation and redemption. You may also want to find a hymnal and look up and meditate on the words to one of these hymns: "Amazing Grace," "Jesus Paid It All," or "The Old Rugged Cross."

NOTE: If you do not know what I mean by salvation, please read my personal salvation story in the appendix.

Putting On Joy: Day 5

But the fruit of the Spirit is love, **JOY***, peace, longsuffering, gentleness, goodness, faith, meekness, temperance: against such there is no law.* (Galatians 5:22–23)

I trust you were blessed as you rejoiced in your salvation throughout the day yesterday. Today we're going to look at the third of the great sources of joy, one that we may choose to be clothed in as often as we wish!

3. **There is joy in praising the Lord.**

Take some time to read the following Psalms. Don't worry— they're short. In your notebook or workbook, write down at least one verse from each chapter that seems to sum up the author's message.

Psalm 66
Psalm 67
Psalm 81
Psalm 95
Psalm 100

These five chapters are only a handful of the many passages in the Bible that talk about praising the Lord *on purpose*. When we make a *conscious effort* to praise God, it is amazing how our attitude improves!

We have one CD at our house that has been dubbed "the morning CD." Many mornings when we are moving slowly or having a hard time being pleasant, I will put on that CD and play the song "I Will Joyfully Sing." As we listen to the words or sing along and *choose* to praise our Savior, it never fails to reset the paths of our selfish hearts to praise mode.

As you finish your quiet time today, make a list of ten things about God or things God has done for you for which you can praise him.

Putting On Joy: Day 6

But the fruit of the Spirit is love, **JOY**, *peace, longsuffering, gentleness, goodness, faith, meekness, temperance: against such there is no law.* (Galatians 5:22–23)

If spending time with, thinking about, and praising our Savior aren't enough, there are even more ways to put on joy in our day-to-day routines.

4. There is joy in sharing.

Write out Nehemiah 8:10 in your notebook or workbook.

God's people were to enjoy the blessings he had provided for them and to share them with those less fortunate *without being sorry* about it! When you and I *choose* to put off the cape of selfishness and put on the Spirit by sharing God's blessings with those around us, it brings joy.

5. There is joy in loving others.

Read John 15:9–13 and answer the following questions:
1. What is the main point of the passage?
2. What does the passage tell us about God's character?

In days 1–3 of the study, we learned that love is an action. This passage tells us that if we are of the Father, we will love as he loves, even to the point of laying down our lives for another. In *choosing* to love and acting out our love to others, our joy will be *full*.

6. **There is joy in weakness.**

This is the one that seems a true paradox to me. Aren't we supposed to be strong Supermoms? How can we find joy in being weak?

Write out 2 Corinthians 12:9.

The answer to the above question is this:

> When we *choose* to maintain a right attitude
> and to recognize God as the strength-giving God
> of our present circumstance,
> and when we recognize that
> he lovingly arranged this circumstance
> so that he can walk with us through it,
> *that realization* brings joy.

As you finish your ten minutes today, I want to challenge you to prayerfully answer the following questions:
1. What has God given you that you can share with others today?
2. Choose one person to whom you will show God's love in action today. Write down their name and what you plan to do.
3. What situation in your life today has God lovingly arranged so that you can have joy because he is walking with you through it?
4. Will you choose to put on joy?

Putting On Peace: Day 7

But the fruit of the Spirit is love, joy, **PEACE***, longsuffering, gentleness, goodness, faith, meekness, temperance: against such there is no law.* (Galatians 5:22–23)

Putting on our capes and proclaiming ourselves Supermoms may ensure a temporary peace (or at least law and order) in our homes, but it does not ensure peace of mind or heart.

That kind of peace is a result of choices you and I make in our beliefs and in our thinking.

When we choose to believe lies (of the devil or of the world) and choose to meditate on those lies, our hearts responds with tumult and fear. We must make a conscious decision to choose peace, and then follow God's directions to keep our minds and hearts stayed on him.

Today, let's dwell on two things that allow us to know true peace, even in the midst of life's most difficult circumstances:

1. **Forgiveness from sin.**

Living at peace with God brings peace. We need no longer fear, for God through Christ has forgiven us.

Read Luke 7:48–50.

Close proximity to the one who created the wind and waves and ultimately controls the storm brings peace in the midst of the storm. Unconfessed sin creates distance between us and our Father God. The further we are from him, the less peaceful our hearts.

In the same way that a broken promise or disobedience would create a problem with the relationship between a child and her earthly parents, so sin creates a problem in our relationship with God. When we confess our sins (and he promises to forgive when we confess—1 John 1:9), the barrier is removed and we enjoy the closeness, security, and peace once more.

2. **Living at peace with others.**

Write out Hebrews 12:14–15 in your notebook or workbook.

When there is sin, misunderstanding, or hurt between us and another person, it is also a hindrance to peace. How much better to live right with God and right with men, as much as possible.

Use the last few minutes of your quiet time today to prayerfully answer the following questions:

1. Is there any sin that you have not yet confessed to the Lord and asked his forgiveness for? If so, please take care of that before you finish your quiet time today.
2. Is there anyone you have wronged or have you created any miscommunications or hurt feelings with another person and not yet sought their forgiveness? I encourage you to write down their name and a date by which you commit to taking care of this in person.

Putting On Peace: Day 8

*But the fruit of the Spirit is love, joy, **PEACE**, longsuffering, gentleness, goodness, faith, meekness, temperance: against such there is no law.* (Galatians 5:22–23)

How often do we moms strap on our Supermom capes and do everything in our power to control a situation? And how many of those times are we stressing and worrying over a situation that is completely out of our hands? Control and manipulation of people and circumstances bring only turmoil and more stress.

God wants us to consciously put on peace by trusting in him. He is bigger than all our problems, fears, and insecurities. Look up the following verses and write them in your own words in your notebook or workbook.

Isaiah 26:3–4
Psalm 84:11–12
Ruth 2:12
Psalm 37:40
Psalm 118:8–9

As you finish today, take a moment to read back through the verses you just wrote and prayerfully answer the following questions:
1. What do these verses tell you about yourself?
2. What do they tell you about God and his character?
3. What do you plan to do based on what you have learned about peace and trust today?

Putting On Peace: Day 9

But the fruit of the Spirit is love, joy, **PEACE**, *longsuffering, gentleness, goodness, faith, meekness, temperance: against such there is no law.* (Galatians 5:22–23)

Read John 14:27.

God promises us peace—the opposite of fear—but it comes as a result of certain actions.

Write out Psalm 119:165 in your notebook or workbook.

Do you love God's Word? How much time do you spend in it compared to doing other things you really enjoy?

With knowledge comes power. When we spend time in God's Word, we come to know him better. A young wife gets to know her husband by spending time with him, studying him, and learning from him, of him, and about him. Likewise, we get to know God and increase our power to defeat the enemy through God's strength by spending time in his Word, studying it, and learning from it.

Write out 2 Peter 1:2.

Knowing God is the best way to find peace. The more you know him, the more you trust him, and the more you understand his love, forgiveness, and adoption, the more peace you have. Peace is multiplied to you.

Take the last few minutes of your time today to list things that you know about God. What is he like? What is his character? What has he done? What is he doing? What does he like? What does he hate? What has he promised to his children?

May you put on peace by increasing your knowledge of God today.

Putting On Longsuffering: Day 10

But the fruit of the Spirit is love, joy, peace, **LONGSUFFERING**, *gentleness, goodness, faith, meekness, temperance: against such there is no law.* (Galatians 5:22–23)

Because we desire to appear to the world as Supermoms who have it all under control and never suffer setbacks or failures or difficulties, sometimes it is hard to know how to handle suffering in a spiritually mature way.

I don't know about you, but for me, longsuffering raised a few questions: What kind of longsuffering does a mom have to endure? How can a mother have and live the character of longsuffering? What exactly is longsuffering anyway? It can't possibly mean *to suffer long*, can it?

Read 2 Corinthians 1:5–7 and answer the following questions in your notebook or workbook:
1. How do these verses describe longsuffering?

Read Psalm 86:15.

2. What else is in the list right along with longsuffering?

What things might a mother be called upon to suffer in a patient, compassionate, merciful, and gracious way?

Suffering as a result of sin
Suffering from physical afflictions
Suffering loss (physical losses, death of a loved one or child, loss of job or position, loss of home and goods, etc.)
Suffering because of a lack of conveniences (such as missionaries face)
Suffering at the hands of a loved one
Suffering inflicted by enemies (mocking, pressures, threats, etc.)

Can you think of others?

Spend the last few minutes of your quiet time asking the Lord to help you put off the Supermom cape of "everything is fine" and endure your hardships with his strength and grace.

Putting On Longsuffering: Day 11

But the fruit of the Spirit is love, joy, peace, **LONGSUFFERING**, *gentleness, goodness, faith, meekness, temperance: against such there is no law.* (Galatians 5:22–23)

The bad news: Life has seasons of longsuffering.

The good news: God will help. We don't have to be the Supermom in every situation because God is a Super God and has promised us his help!

Write out Philippians 4:11–13 in your notebook or workbook.

More good news: God is faithful.

Write out 1 Corinthians 10:13.

In your notebook or workbook, describe some situation in which God has sovereignly placed you to suffer for his sake.

As you finish your quiet time, read back through those verses you wrote out today. Ask God to help you identify and make a list of the ways he is helping you and is being faithful to you in the midst of this God-ordained suffering.

Putting On Longsuffering: Day 12

But the fruit of the Spirit is love, joy, peace, **LONGSUFFERING***, gentleness, goodness, faith, meekness, temperance: against such there is no law.* (Galatians 5:22–23)

Remember the good news from yesterday: God will help, and God is faithful!

Today there is even more good news: In addition to his help and faithfulness, we can find comfort in God's promises and in his laws (the Word of God).

Write out Psalm 119:49–52 in your notebook or workbook.

Now find and write out at least three other verses that state God's promises to you or that comfort you.

Spend the rest of your quiet time today talking with the Lord. You may choose to use the prayer below, or you may wish to just talk to him using your own heart's cry.

Lord, help me to live longsuffering in a way that pleases you. Help me to be lovingly patient with my family and with others, whether they are patient with me or not. Allow my heart to recognize and be at peace with your sovereign control over my circumstances. If you allow suffering, and if you allow it to be long, please help me by your Spirit to endure it with a grace that will bring you glory. Amen.

Putting On Gentleness: Day 13

But the fruit of the Spirit is love, joy, peace, longsuffering, **GENTLENESS***, goodness, faith, meekness, temperance: against such there is no law.* (Galatians 5:22–23)

The Merriam-Webster dictionary defines *gentleness* as this: *The quality or state of being gentle*

And *gentle* is defined this way: *Having or showing a kind and quiet nature*

Based on those definitions, we could say that gentleness = quiet kindness.

When we look at the life of Christ, we see that whether he was blessing children, teaching multitudes, facing criticism, or being unjustly put to death, he was the perfect example of gentleness, kindness, and quiet responses.

Read what Jesus had to say about kindness in the life of a believer in Luke 6:27–38.

If you write in your Bible, I encourage you to mark all the action words that show gentleness or kindness, and then list them in your notebook or workbook.

As you finish your quiet time, ask the Lord to help you actively put off the Supermom cape of selfishness and self-preservation and put on his gentleness and kindness today. Go down through the list you just made and pray specifically about ways you can do/be/show _____ to your children, your husband, and anyone else the Lord brings to mind.

Putting On Gentleness: Day 14

But the fruit of the Spirit is love, joy, peace, longsuffering, **GENTLENESS**, *goodness, faith, meekness, temperance: against such there is no law.* (Galatians 5:22–23)

Read Luke 6:27–38 again. Be sure to note the action words.

Love, do good, bless, pray, give, do, love, lend, love, do good, lend, be merciful, judge not, condemn not, forgive, give.

Did you notice all the action words in there? Being gentle and showing kindness is a choice. It is love in action. We choose to show God's kindness (or not) by a thousand different actions we take every day.

Yesterday we prayed over the specific things we can do that we might not normally do to show gentleness and kindness to our family and others. Today, I want you to make a list of those names in your notebook or workbook. Then write out what you will do to show special kindness to each one. Give yourself a deadline if you need to, and ask God to give you his strength to follow through.

Superheroes are fictional. Your family needs you to be real and to be kind for them for them today. By God's grace, one day they will remember you as the gentlest and kindest woman they ever met. God is pleased and his name is praised when we clothe ourselves in his gentleness.

Putting On Goodness: Day 15

But the fruit of the Spirit is love, joy, peace, longsuffering, gentleness, **GOODNESS***, faith, meekness, temperance: against such there is no law.* (Galatians 5:22–23)

> *Being right does not equal being good.*

Think about that statement for a moment.

In the world of modern-day Supermoms, it is easy to view goodness in terms of rightness. We tend to think like this:

> I am always right; therefore I am a good mom.
> A good mom is always right.
> A good mom always makes the right decisions for her kids.
> A good mom doesn't make mistakes.

These are lies of the enemy that we have chosen to believe, and they are damaging us and our families. These lies are what cause so many of us to rely on the false security of the capes of our own goodness or our own wisdom.

Write out the following verses in your notebook or workbook.

Psalm 53:3
Romans 5:19

2 Corinthians 5:21

The truth is that we can be *good* only through the forgiveness and grace of God. And the wisdom to be *right* must also come from him and his goodness flowing to us.

Write out James 1:5 and then answer the following questions:
  1. What must we do to obtain God's wisdom?
  2. When we ask him for it, what is his promise?

Putting on his goodness and wisdom and allowing them to flow through us will have a much greater impact on our families than any fleshly goodness or worldly wisdom we could offer on our own.

Spend the last few minutes of your quiet time today reflecting on your personal relationship with the Lord. If you need his forgiveness for something in order to be right with him, take care of that now, and then humbly ask him for his goodness and wisdom for your day. He promises to give them.

Putting On Goodness: Day 16

*But the fruit of the Spirit is love, joy, peace, longsuffering, gentleness, **GOODNESS**, faith, meekness, temperance: against such there is no law.* (Galatians 5:22–23)

Today, let's take off the Supermom cape of "being right = being good" and take a few minutes to look at goodness in light of love, another fruit of the Spirit.

Read Galatians 5:21–23.

Now go back and reread 1 Corinthians 13.

In your notebook or workbook, write down some of the ways that God shows his goodness and love in action to us as believers and to you personally.

Spend the last few minutes of your quiet time today in prayer. Ask the Lord to help you recognize his goodness to you today. Ask him to help you imitate his goodness in your life and share that goodness with your children, your husband, and others whom God brings across your path.

Putting On Goodness: Day 17

But the fruit of the Spirit is love, joy, peace, longsuffering, gentleness, **GOODNESS***, faith, meekness, temperance: against such there is no law.* (Galatians 5:22–23)

When we wear the Supermom cape of our own wisdom, we sometimes tend to think that being a good mom means having it all together, never getting flustered, keeping a spotless house, or having perfectly behaved children. A good mom in God's eyes may appear to do those things, but much more is involved.

When we look at goodness from the biblical perspective of love in action, this is what Supermom goodness may really look like:

> *When they hide,*
> *You find them.*
> *When their behavior is unlovely,*
> *You love them.*
> *When training is hard,*
> *You do the hard thing.*
> *When they stumble and fall,*
> *You pick them up*
> *And kiss their hurts.*
> *When they cry during the night,*
> *You comfort them.*
> *When you want to give up,*
> *You remember God's Word*

That strengthens and encourages you.
When their friends are mean,
You show them compassion.
When the world is cruel,
You show them mercy.
With each "when" in the lives of your children,
You experience God's goodness;
You exemplify God's goodness;
You teach them to trust his goodness.
~ Katie Hornor

Write out Psalm 34:8 in your notebook or workbook and underline the word *good*.

Write out Titus 2:3–5 and underline the word *good*.

According to these verses, who is good?

Our responsibility as women is to be good and to teach others to be good—not as a matter of pride or to show that we are better than anyone else, but so that God, his Word, and his testimony among men are not blasphemed or shamed in any way. That's right—God's testimony is impacted by our goodness or lack thereof. But don't forget his promise to help you do and be what he has called you to do and be.

Write out 1 Thessalonians 5:24.

Wow! It's not about us and our goodness. It's about him! He wants you and me to be good and to show goodness for the sake of his testimony, and he promises to make it happen. We just have to let him.

Spend the last few moments of your quiet time today talking with your Super God. Thank him that you can be confident in his goodness today. Ask him to help you put on true godly goodness that you know you can't do on your own and that will improve his testimony in the world.

Putting On Faith: Day 18

But the fruit of the Spirit is love, joy, peace, longsuffering, gentleness, goodness, **FAITH**, *meekness, temperance: against such there is no law.* (Galatians 5:22–23)

The Merriam-Webster dictionary definition of *faith* (noun) is this:
1. *Strong belief or trust in someone or something, belief in the existence of God, strong religious feelings or beliefs, a system of religious beliefs*
2. *Allegiance to duty or a person, loyalty*
3. *Fidelity to one's promises, sincerity of intentions*
4. *Belief and trust in and loyalty to God, belief in the traditional doctrines of a religion*
5. *Firm belief in something for which there is no proof, complete trust*
6. *Something that is believed especially with strong conviction; especially a system of religious beliefs*

And the definition of *faithful* (adjective) is this:
1. *Adhering firmly and devotedly, as to a person, cause, or idea; loyal*
2. *Engaging in an emotional and sexual relationship only with one's spouse*
3. *Having or full of faith*
4. *Worthy of trust or belief; reliable*
5. *Consistent with truth or actuality*

Who knew faith could have so many meanings?

The first definition we'll look at is faith as devotion or loyalty to Jesus Christ.

Read 2 Peter 1:4–9.

Peter tells us in this passage that we are partakers of the divine nature and that we have escaped the corruption that is in the world.

In your notebook or workbook, write out the seven things that Peter tells us we need to add to our faith so that we can be fruitful in the knowledge of Christ.

Every superhero has a cause. Ask yourself: *Whose cause am I serving? My own? Or am I devoted to my Lord and his cause?*

What is God's cause? Read Mark 16:15.

Going into all the world to preach the Gospel begins in our own homes with the children and visitors God sends us and the other people we come into contact with throughout the course of the day.

> We can put on faithfulness by sharing his message of salvation, redemption, adoption, and hope daily.

> We can remain devoted to him and his purposes for our lives instead of being resistant to the ~~interruptions~~ opportunities he sends our way.

> We can strive to reflect back on him the glory he deserves in everything we do.

As you finish your quiet time today, ask the Lord to help you be loyal to him, his cause, and his sovereign design for your day and for your life. Ask him to help you identify and respond willingly to the opportunities he sends your way to further his cause today.

Putting On Faith: Day 19

But the fruit of the Spirit is love, joy, peace, longsuffering, gentleness, goodness, **FAITH**, *meekness, temperance: against such there is no law.* (Galatians 5:22–23)

The second definition for faith that we want to study is *engaging in an emotional and sexual relationship only with one's spouse.*

NOTE: Dear mom, if you find yourself unmarried today, I encourage you to read today's thoughts with the idea that God is your husband. Before continuing, please read Isaiah 54:4–6 and be encouraged. Then replace the word husband *in today's devotion with the word* Lord.

Marriage was designed and instituted by God as a holy relationship. It is not meant merely for procreation, nor merely for pleasure, but also to be another witness to the world of God's love relationship with his people.

Read Mark 10:6–12 and Ephesians 5:15–33.

Each of us can put on faithfulness to our Lord, enhancing his testimony in the world, by remaining faithful to our husband emotionally, sexually, and relationally.

Ask yourself: *Am I loyal to my husband?*

With God's help, each of us can guard our hearts from emotional affairs. We can consciously and consistently seek to put our husband's needs before our own. We can seek to please him, to make him a priority in our day and in life, know him, defend him, respect him, honor him, and be his most loyal fan.

If you find yourself clothed in the Supermom cape of independence or if you find yourself estranged from your husband, ask the Lord to help you put off that cape and put on faithfulness.

If you feel you are loyal to your husband in every way, ask the Lord to show you areas in which you can improve. Often our hearts deceive us (see Jeremiah 17:9–10), but the Spirit can point out our weak areas and, by his strength, help us gain victory.

If you would like more information and or help concerning husband/wife relationships, you may also want to read 1 Corinthians 7 or see the list of recommended books on the subject at http://paradisepraises.com/freedownloads.

Putting On Faith: Day 20

But the fruit of the Spirit is love, joy, peace, longsuffering, gentleness, goodness, **FAITH***, meekness, temperance: against such there is no law.* (Galatians 5:22–23)

Today we're looking at another definition of faith: *having or full of faith.*

Ask yourself: *Am I full of faith in my Lord?*

Read Hebrews 11:1–2.

According to these verses, faith is *confidence in what we hope for and assurance about what we do not see.* This is what our forefathers in the faith were commended for.

A modern-day Supermom will be tempted to boast in her self-sufficiency. Putting on faith requires that we put off our cape of self-sufficiency and declare our dependence upon and trust in the Lord. We must be full of faith in our God.

Write out Philippians 1:6 in your notebook or workbook.

We can be confident that he who began his good work in us will complete it.

Write out Isaiah 55:8–9.
Write out Jeremiah 29:11.

We can be confident that he knows the plans he has for us and that his ways are better than our ways. Our forefathers were commended for an evident faith, a faith that acted upon their confidence in God.

Ask yourself: *How well do I know God? How confident am I in his sovereignty and perfect plan? How faith-full (full of faith) am I?*

If you are struggling today with trusting God, and being confident of his work in your life, why not tell him that? Like the Father in Mark 9:14–27, you too can cry, *Lord, I believe; help thou mine unbelief.* And he will!

Take the last few minutes of your quiet time today to pour out your heart to your faithful God.

Putting On Faith: Day 21

But the fruit of the Spirit is love, joy, peace, longsuffering, gentleness, goodness, **FAITH**, *meekness, temperance: against such there is no law.* (Galatians 5:22–23)

The fourth definition of faith that we want to look at is *worthy of trust or belief; reliable.*

Based on his own true testimony in his Word, we know that God is faithful and that he is worthy of our trust and belief.

Read Deuteronomy 7:9, Isaiah 25:1, 1 Corinthians 1:9, 1 Corinthians 10:13, and Hebrews 13:8.

Write out Ephesians 5:1 in your notebook or your workbook.

The word *follower* in this verse means *imitator*.

If we are to be followers (imitators) of God, and God is faithful (trustworthy, reliable), then we must also be trustworthy and reliable.

Take a few moments to pray over and answer the following questions:

    1. Do other people see me as a person worthy of trust? Believable? Reliable?

2. Can I be trusted to do what I say I will do?
3. Can I be trusted by my husband and by my children to put high priority on their welfare?
4. Can I be trusted to be consistent, to be responsible, to be dependable, to be approachable because I am allowing God through his Spirit to evidence that fruit in my life?

Putting On Faith: Day 22

But the fruit of the Spirit is love, joy, peace, longsuffering, gentleness, goodness, **FAITH**, *meekness, temperance: against such there is no law.* (Galatians 5:22–23)

The last definition of faith that we will look at is *consistent with truth or actuality.*

Today's question to ponder is this: *Is my life faithful to or consistent with God's principles for living?*

The truth is that you and I *can* live the Truth of God's Word and his principles. Not by donning the Supermom cape of our own strength. Not by tightening the Supermom bootstraps of our own power, but through God's Spirit.

In your notebook or workbook, write out the word of the Lord to Zerubbabel in Zechariah 4:6.

Then write out 1 Thessalonians 5:24.
Write out Matthew 19:26.
Write out 1 John 4:4.
Write out Philippians 4:13.

If God has called us to put on faith and all the other fruits (and he has!), then he will, by his Spirit, give us all we need to accomplish what he has asked of us. We must put off the Supermom cape of pride and self-sufficiency, and choose to put on faithfulness by the help of his Spirit and for his glory.

As you finish your quiet time today, read back through the verses you wrote out and prayerfully answer the following questions:
1. What do these verses tell you about yourself?
2. What do they tell you about God and his character?
3. What changes do you plan to make based on what you have learned about God's faithfulness and your current level of faithfulness to him?

May you live in the victory of faithfulness today!

Putting On Meekness: Day 23

But the fruit of the Spirit is love, joy, peace, longsuffering, gentleness, goodness, faith, **MEEKNESS***, temperance: against such there is no law.* (Galatians 5:22–23)

Meekness is one of the harder fruits of the Spirit to discuss because in the course of the many translations of Scripture since Jesus' time on earth, I fear we have lost its true meaning.

We tend to equate meekness with weakness or cowardliness. We tend to think of a meek person as one who takes whatever is given to him without protest, without protecting his own rights, or as someone who allows himself to be stepped upon and used by others. The problem with that definition, however, is that Jesus Christ was none of those things.

Read Matthew 5:1–12.

In the context of Matthew 5, the Sermon on the Mount, meekness appears to be the expression of the two previous beatitudes in the list. What are those two beatitudes? Write them down in your notebook or workbook.

Write out Matthew 5:3–5.

As you finish your quiet time today, spend some time rereading Matthew 5:1–12 and ask the Lord to show you what it means to be poor in spirit, to mourn, and to be meek as he is meek.

Putting On Meekness: Day 24

But the fruit of the Spirit is love, joy, peace, longsuffering, gentleness, goodness, faith, **MEEKNESS**, *temperance: against such there is no law.* (Galatians 5:22–23)

Reread Matthew 5:1–12.
Read Romans 12:3.

We understand *poor in spirit* to mean *humble*, or as Romans 12:3 says, "not to think of himself more highly than he ought to think, but to think soberly" [in a self-restrained manner].

Bible scholars believe that the phrase *those who mourn* refers to those who mourn over their sin, agree with God about the wicked wretchedness of their disobedience, and display a godly sorrow over their rebellion toward him and his will.

We could say that meekness is
> *the combination of the inward realization and outward expression of humbleness and sorrow for sin.*

We might say that meekness is humbly admitting that we deserve nothing but eternal punishment in and of our own merits, and therefore whatever God, by his grace, gives to us is a blessing!

This realization creates in us repentant hearts out of which should flow gratefulness and hopefulness, regardless of the God-ordained circumstances in which we find ourselves.

Write out Titus 3:3–7 in your notebook or workbook.

Spend the last few minutes of your quiet time today thinking about your own unworthiness and praising and thanking God for his Son and for the great and undeserved gift of forgiveness and salvation from eternal punishment.

You may also want to find a hymnal and look up and meditate on the words to the hymn "Grace Greater Than Our Sin."

NOTE: If you do not understand what I mean by salvation, please read my personal story of salvation in the <u>appendix</u>.

Putting On Meekness: Day 25

But the fruit of the Spirit is love, joy, peace, longsuffering, gentleness, goodness, faith, **MEEKNESS**, *temperance: against such there is no law.* (Galatians 5:22–23)

So if meekness is humbly admitting that we deserve nothing in and of our own merits but eternal punishment, and realizing that because what we deserve is eternal punishment therefore whatever God, by his grace, gives to us is a blessing . . . how should we respond to that?

Read Isaiah 6:5 and answer the following question in your notebook or workbook.
How did Isaiah respond when he saw himself for who he was and saw God for who he is?

Write out Psalm 84:10–12.
Write out Psalm 9:1–2.

The next time your day is ranking 1 out of 10 on the Supermom charts, take some time to humble your heart before the Lord. Take off your self-righteous Supermom cape and remember who you are, where God found you, what you really deserve, and what he rescued you from. Then realize that even this day, hard though it is, is a blessing from him. And praise him for it!

Read Psalm 40:1–17.

The next step: Teach your children how to be meek, how to come to the same realization. Teach them about their wretched sinfulness and need of the Savior and the good news that God is willing to forgive them, to love them, to adopt them, and to treat them better than they deserve!

As you finish your quiet time today, spend a few moments praising the Lord and a few moments interceding on behalf of your children.

Ask God to help you recognize those moments in your day when your child is open to the Gospel and to give you the wisdom and words to lead his or her heart toward salvation. If you would like more information or help concerning sharing the Gospel with your child, see the list of recommended books under the heading "parenting/child training" at http://paradisepraises.com/freedownloads.

Putting On Temperance: Day 26

But the fruit of the Spirit is love, joy, peace, longsuffering, gentleness, goodness, faith, meekness, **TEMPERANCE**: *against such there is no law.* (Galatians 5:22–23)

Self-control is a more modern word for *temperance*. The Merriam-Webster dictionary online gives us these definitions:

Self-control: restraint exercised over one's own impulses, emotions, or desires

Temperance: a. moderation in action, thought, or feeling: restraint; b. habitual moderation in the indulgence of the appetites or passions

It's interesting that the word translated *temperance* in Galatians 5:22-23 can be found in other Bible versions in conjunction with such things as vulnerability, righteousness, intimacy, athletics, gentleness, modesty, patience, and leadership.

Self-protection is the enemy of self-control. When we try to protect ourselves, we give in to our own emotion of fear and indulge in trying to control everything around us.

When we refuse to lay aside the Supermom cape of self-protection and put on the Spirit in the area of self-control the following things may happen:

We may sacrifice being righteous for being right.

We may endanger the intimacy in our marriages.

We may create our own health issues.

We may hurt those we love most by our lack of gentleness in speech and touch.

We may justify our own definition of modesty instead of the Lord's.

We may lose patience and raise our voices—yes, even yell at times.

We may, by our lack of self-control, cause our children to disrespect or even resent our leadership.

We justify our self-protection and try hard to keep our capes in place, not realizing that our appearance is more that of a control monster than a spirit-filled mom. But the good news is that God has not given us a spirit of fear.

Read Romans 8:31–39.

In your notebook or workbook, write out 2 Timothy 1:7.

The feeling of vulnerability and the need for self-protection and controlling everything and everyone around us stems from fear.

As you finish your quiet time today, take some time to prayerfully consider the above passages and answer the following questions:
1. What is my biggest fear? What do I fear the most?
2. Why do I fear it?
3. Does the fear come from me? From the devil or the world? Or from God?
4. Can anything separate me from the love of God?

Putting On Temperance: Day 27

But the fruit of the Spirit is love, joy, peace, longsuffering, gentleness, goodness, faith, meekness, **TEMPERANCE**: *against such there is no law.* (Galatians 5:22–23)

Yesterday we talked about how lack of temperance, or self-control, is really an effort to control based on our fears. If you need to, go back and reread Romans 8:31–39, and spend a few minutes rejoicing in the fact that nothing can separate us from God's love.

God's love is so vast that it actually makes us perfect and casts out fear.

Read 1 John 4:10–18.

Write out 1 John 4:18 in your notebook or workbook.

God wants to help us have self-control, and he is never more pleased to answer our prayers than when we pray for something that is according to his will.

We already know from Galatians 5:22–23 that self-control is his will for every believer, so it follows naturally that God will help us in the area of self-control if we ask him to. Why? Because it brings him glory!

Write out John 14:13–14.

Now read back through the verses you just wrote and prayerfully answer the following questions:

1. What do these verses tell you about yourself?
2. What do they tell you about God and his character?
3. What do you plan to do based on what you have learned about God's love and self-control today?

Finish up your quiet time by asking the Lord to help you put off the cape of fear and control and to put on self-control by the power of his Spirit. Then be conscious of his help throughout the day and be mindful to give him glory for doing through you what you could not do on your own.

The Whole Fruit: Day 28

But the fruit of the Spirit is love, joy, peace, longsuffering, gentleness, goodness, faith, meekness, temperance: against such there is no law. (Galatians 5:22–23)

We have now covered all of the fruit of the Spirit on the list. Have you noticed as we've gone through this study that each time we singled out a fruit, we almost always mentioned another fruit in conjunction with it? Coincidence? I don't think so.

There is a reason it is called the fruit (singular) of the Spirit. Love, joy, peace, longsuffering, gentleness, goodness, faith, meekness, and temperance are not separate fruits but all a part of one fruit.

This is not a fruit-basket life where we can pick and choose which part of Christlikeness we want to put on. No, this is more like an orange, where each virtue is a different slice of the orange. You must have all the slices together and in their places to have a whole, complete orange.

Having some of all of these characteristics in your life is outward proof of the indwelling of God's Spirit, which takes place at the time of salvation and adoption.

God said:
> The greatest virtue is love (1 Corinthians 13:13).
> There is no greater proof of love than to lay down your life for a friend (John 15:13).

His love constrains (compels) us (2 Corinthians 5:14).

So love, then, may be the fibers that hold all the slices together, but without peace, there is no joy. Without goodness, there is no gentleness. Without self-control there is no longsuffering. Without faith, there is no meekness. Do you see how it all fits together?

We cannot build a Christian life on these fruits one at a time, waiting to master one and then moving on to the next. It doesn't work that way. We must (with God's promised assistance) put on the singular fruit of all of these God-honoring characteristics together, and at the same time.

Sound overwhelming?

Remember God's promises.

Write out 1 Thessalonians 5:24 in your notebook or workbook.
Write out Philippians 1:6.
Write out Philippians 4:13.

A mom who is super in God's eyes will recognize the futility of her own disguises and will put off the cape of her own abilities in humble awe of her all-powerful, sovereign Savior and in favor of putting on the fruit of his Spirit.

Moment by moment.

Day by day.

And by doing so, she will not only glorify her Creator, but she will also become a legend in her own time and leave behind a hero's legacy that glorifies the God whose Spirit makes that life possible.

What will you do, Supermom?

Will you hide behind your cape?

Or will you lay down the cape, take the leap of faith, and with God's help be a Spirit-filled hero for the Lord?

I am praying you choose the second one.

Thank you for studying through *Putting On the Spirit* with me. If you have enjoyed it, won't you please take a moment to leave a review of the book at your favorite ebook retailer? And please tell your friends that they can get their own copy at www.ParadisePraises.com!

Putting On the Spirit is also available in Spanish at www.Lemonhass.com as *Vistiéndose del Espíritu*.

Thanks so much!
Katie Hornor

Appendix

If you do not know what I mean when I talk about repentance, salvation, redemption, or adoption, I hope you'll take a moment to let me tell you my story and explain what I mean.

I am adopted, and in the future I am going to live in a mansion built for me by my Father, the King. I will enjoy banquets and great choirs surrounded by gold and jewels. Best of all, I will bask in his smile. How do I know all this? He told me. And he told me that he has many mansions and that anyone who wants to may become his child and enjoy these treasures for eternity. Sounds like a fairy tale, doesn't it?

My Father is God. Here is the story of how I met him and became his child and heir through adoption.

His story started long before mine. Way back when he first created the world and set the stars in their places, he knew about me, loved me, and provided for my future adoption. When I began to learn about who he is, I realized that I had sinned against him, who is God, is holy, and cannot stand sin.

> *For all have sinned, and come short of the glory of God* (Romans 3:23).

I realized that every one of us does sinful things that offend God and for which we deserve punishment. In the end, all of my sins are sins against the Eternal God, and therefore only an eternal punishment is sufficient.

> *For the wages [payment] of sin is death; but the gift of God is eternal life through Jesus Christ our Lord* (Romans 6:23).

The amazing part of the story, though, is that Jesus Christ, the only one without sin (1 Peter 2:22), the eternal Son of God, became a man (John 1:1, 14) and died to pay my penalty—and yours!

> *God commendeth [shows] his love toward us, in that, while we were yet sinners, Christ died for us* (Romans 5:8).

Jesus Christ died on the cross (John 19:31–42), taking upon himself the punishment that you and I deserved (2 Corinthians 5:21). Three days later, he rose from the dead (1 Corinthians 15:1–4), confirming his victory over sin and death.

> *According to his abundant mercy [God] hath begotten us again unto a lively hope by the resurrection of Jesus Christ from the dead* (1 Peter 1:3).

By faith, I needed to change my thinking about Jesus Christ, who he is, what he did for my salvation, and why (Acts 3:19). I found out that if I put my faith (trust, confidence) in him, trusting in his death on the cross for my sins, he will forgive me and promises me eternal life in Heaven. And he will do the same for you!

> *For God so loved the world, that he gave his only begotten Son, that whosoever believeth in him should not perish, but have everlasting life* (John 3:16).
> *If thou shalt confess with thy mouth the Lord Jesus and shalt believe in thine heart that God hath raised Him from the dead, thou shalt be saved* (Romans 10:9).

Faith in the finished work of Jesus Christ on the cross is the only true way to be adopted by God and inherit eternal life!

> *For by grace are ye saved through faith; and that not of yourselves: it is the gift of God: Not of works, lest any man should boast* (Ephesians 2:8–9).

If you, like me, desire to accept Jesus Christ as Savior for your sins and to be adopted into God's family for eternity, here is a prayer you can pray. It is important for you to know, however, that saying these specific words or any other prayer is not what does the forgiving, the saving (adopting), and the giving of eternal life. This prayer is simply a way to express to God your faith in him and thank him for the salvation from sin and judgment that he has provided through Jesus Christ.

> "God, I know I have sinned against you and that I deserve punishment. I believe that Jesus Christ took upon himself the punishment that I deserved so that by faith in him I can be forgiven. I put my trust in you for salvation from sin and its punishment. Thank you for your wonderful grace and forgiveness and for your gift of eternal life and the privilege to be your child. Amen."

If you truly believe this, God's Word says that you have become

> *a new creature: old things are passed away; behold, all things are become new* (2 Corinthians 5:17).

God also says that you are now adopted as his child and have the eternal position of the daughter and heir of God.

> *But as many as received him, to them gave he power to become the sons of God, even to them that believe on his name* (John 1:12; see also Galatians 4:4–6, 1 John 3:1–2).

Have you made a decision to trust Jesus Christ for salvation and eternal life? If you have, or if you would like to know more about salvation, eternal life, or getting to know God as his daughter, please contact me and let me know. I would be happy to help you or to put you in touch with a Bible-believing church in your area that can answer your questions with God's Word.

Love,
Katie

About Katie

 Katie and her husband Tap have been missionaries in tropical Mexico for over 10 years. They homeschool their five children and minister locally as well as through their international hispanic homeschool ministry, lemonhass.com

Katie is a teacher at heart and by trade and loves to encourage women in their God-given roles through speaking, writing and blogging. Katie blogs about marriage, motherhood, and ministry at ParadisePraises.com and teaches bloggers to grow their business to stable online income at BloggingSuccessfully.com

Connect with Katie

Connect with Katie by subscribing to her blog or inviting her to speak at your next event, or you may wish to follow her on Facebook, Pinterest, Twitter, or Instagram.

Other Titles by Katie Hornor

Divine Design: A Study of Feminine Priorities

Loving You Long Distance: Tips for Strengthening Long Distance Family Relationships

Vistiéndose del Espíritu (this book in Spanish)

Melk, The Christmas Monkey - a Christian Alternative to Elf on the Shelf

Christmas Around the World

Shop at www.Shop.ParadisePraises.com

Made in the USA
Monee, IL
22 March 2024

54933605R00042